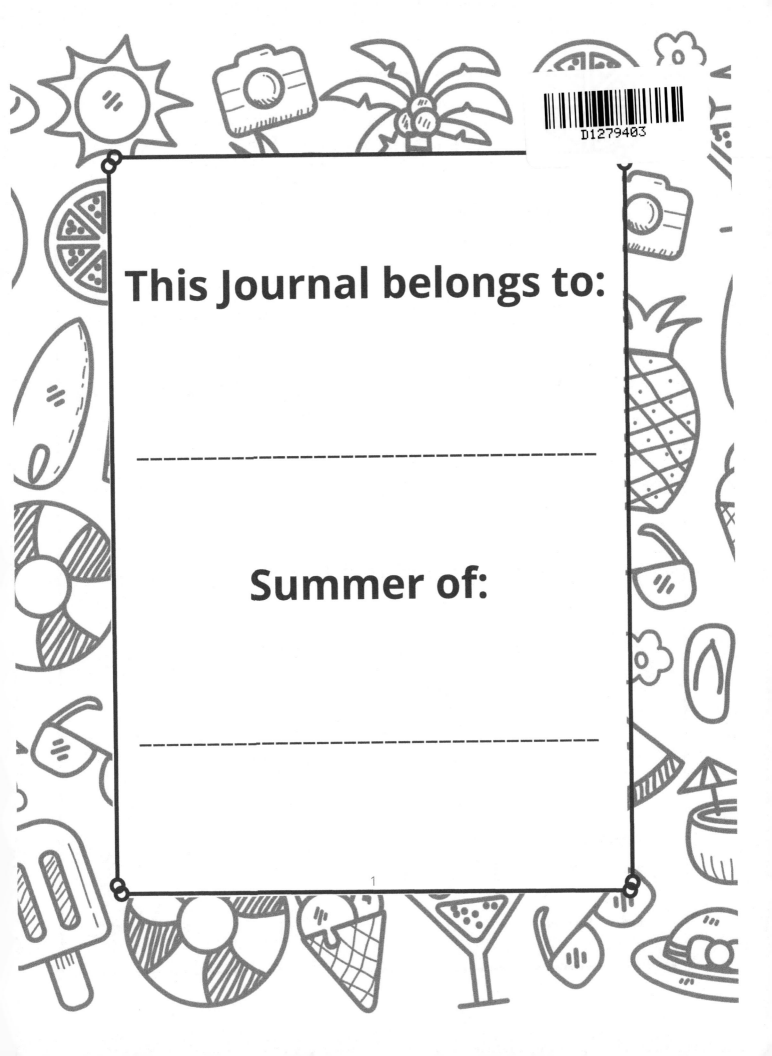

This Journal belongs to:

_____

Summer of:

_____

How to use this Journal:

There is no order. Feel free to skip around.

There are prompts on each page to get you started, but you make the rules! Write, doodle, color, draw or use stickers, pictures, tickets, maps or anything else that holds a memory to capture the moment!

Have fun!

Supplies you need for this Journal

- Markers/pen/pencils
- Scissors
- Glue stick or tape
- Tangible reminders of activities, stickers, ticket stubs, etc.
- Pictures

 # Summer Buket List

- [ ] Pick Berries
- [ ] Have a Lemonade Stand
- [ ] Eat Popsicles
- [ ] Visit The Farmers Market
- [ ] Go to the Pool/Beach
- [ ] Make Ice Cream
- [ ] Fly Kites
- [ ] Watch Fireworks
- [ ] Build a Sandcastle
- [ ] Visit the Zoo
- [ ] Go camping
- [ ] Have a Picnic
- [ ] Nap in a Hammock
- [ ] Run through sprinklers
- [ ] Have a balloon Fight
- [ ] Watch the Sunset
- [ ] Play Frisbee
- [ ] Play freeze Tag
- [ ] Climb a Tree

- [ ] Go on a Bike Ride
- [ ] Draw with sidewalk Chalk
- [ ] Play a Board Game
- [ ] Launch a Model Rocket
- [ ] Catch Lightning Bugs
- [ ] Make Root Beer Floats
- [ ] Take some Photos
- [ ] _____
- [ ] _____
- [ ] _____
- [ ] _____
- [ ] _____
- [ ] _____
- [ ] _____
- [ ] _____
- [ ] _____
- [ ] _____
- [ ] _____
- [ ] _____

Summer Reading Challenge

My Summer Reading Goal:_____

Book Title:

_____   _____
_____   _____
_____   _____
_____   _____
_____   _____
_____   _____
_____   _____
_____   _____
_____   _____
_____   _____
_____   _____
_____   _____
_____   _____

Reading Challenge:

☐ Read a book published this year   ☐ Read a book that is also now a film

☐ Read a book based on a true story   ☐ Read about a historic event

☐ Read a book about the future   ☐ Read a collection of poems

☐ Read a newspaper   ☐ Reread a book you love

Opinion Writing Checklist

Feel free to go back to this page as many time you need.

☐ I used a capital letter at the beginning of sentences and proper nouns.

-**T**he cat is fat.
-My friend is **R**ose, she lives in **F**lorida.

☐ I spelled sight words I know correctly.

Let's **go to my** house.

☐ I sounded out words I didn't know.

c-h-a-r-t

☐ I left spaces between my words.

I ☝ like ☝ candies.

☐ I used punctuation at the end of my sentences.

● ! ?

☐ I stayed on topic.

☐ I wrote my opinion and feelings.

☐ I wrote complete sentences.

☐ I wrote a concluding sentence.

Opinion Writing Ideas

Feel free to go back to this page as many time you need.

Sentences Starters

My favorite
I think
I believe
The best
If I had
I feel

I like
I do not like
I agree
I disagree
In my opinion

Transition Words

First
Second
Third
Next

Another reason
Also
Finally
Last

Writing the Conclusion

As you can see
That is why I believe
It is clear that

All in all
In conclusion
To summarize

My goals for this summer are:

....

....

....

....

....

....

One way I'm going to challenge myself this summer:

....

....

....

....

....

Date:

Weather:

Today I'm feeling:

📍 _____

What I did today:

_____
_____
_____
_____
_____
_____
_____

I'm grateful for: _____

_____

Best thing today: _____

_____

Date:  Weather:

Today I'm feeling:

📍 _____

What I did today:

_____

_____

_____

_____

_____

_____

_____

I'm grateful for: _____

_____

Best thing today: _____

_____

Date: Weather:

Today I'm feeling:

What I did today:

_____

_____

_____

_____

_____

_____

_____

I'm grateful for: _____

_____

Best thing today: _____

_____

Date:

Weather:

Today I'm feeling:

📍 _____

What I did today:

_____
_____
_____
_____
_____
_____
_____

I'm grateful for: _____

_____

Best thing today: _____

_____

Date:

Weather:

Today I'm feeling:

◯ _____

What I did today:

_____

_____

_____

_____

_____

_____

_____

I'm grateful for: _____

_____

Best thing today: _____

_____

Date:

Weather:

Today I'm feeling:

📍 _____

What I did today:

_____
_____
_____
_____
_____
_____
_____

I'm grateful for: _____

_____

Best thing today: _____

_____

Date: **Date:** **Weather:**

Today I'm feeling:

_____

What I did today:

_____

_____

_____

_____

_____

_____

_____

I'm grateful for: _____

_____

Best thing today: _____

_____

Date:

Weather:

Today I'm feeling:

📍 _____

What I did today:

_____
_____
_____
_____
_____
_____
_____
_____

I'm grateful for: _____

_____

Best thing today: _____

_____

Date:

Weather:

Today I'm feeling:

📍 _____

What I did today:

_____

_____

_____

_____

_____

_____

_____

I'm grateful for: _____

_____

Best thing today: _____

_____

What is the most important thing you would like to do this summer?

....

....

....

....

....

Describe your perfect summer day:

....

....

....

....

....

....

....

Date: ___ Weather: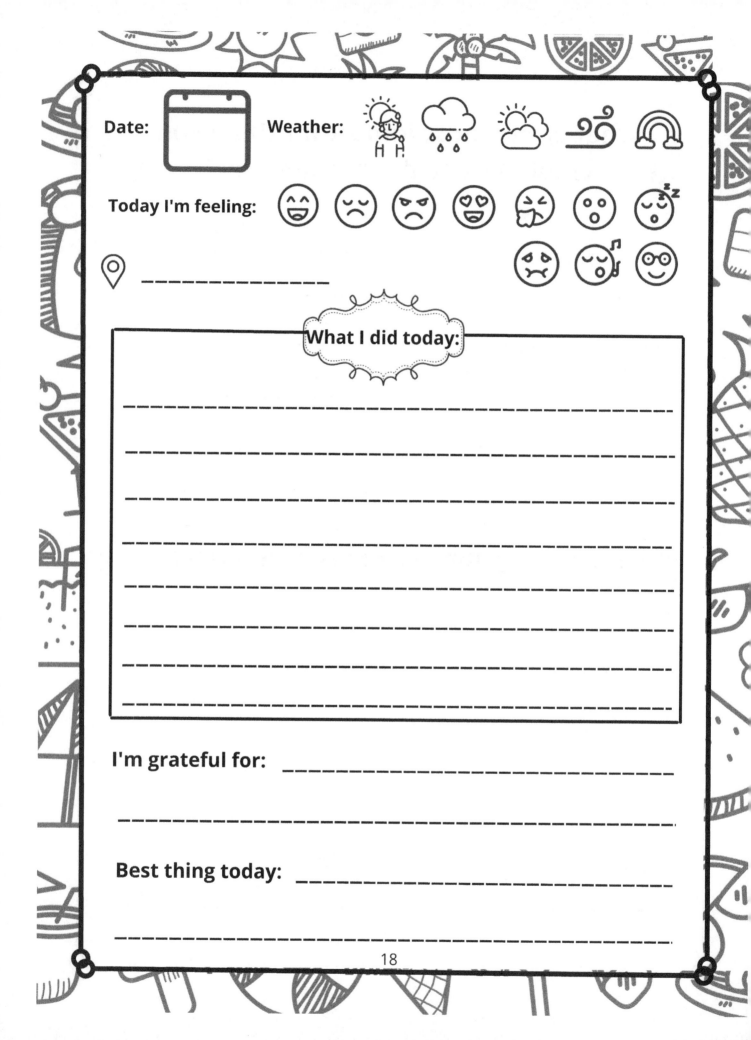

Today I'm feeling:

📍 _____

What I did today:

_____

_____

_____

_____

_____

_____

_____

I'm grateful for: _____

_____

Best thing today: _____

_____

Date:

Weather:

Today I'm feeling:

📍 _____

What I did today:

_____

_____

_____

_____

_____

_____

_____

I'm grateful for: _____

_____

Best thing today: _____

_____

Date: **Weather:**

Today I'm feeling:

_____

What I did today:

_____

_____

_____

_____

_____

_____

_____

I'm grateful for: _____

_____

Best thing today: _____

_____

Date:

Weather:

Today I'm feeling:

📍 _____

What I did today:

_____

_____

_____

_____

_____

_____

_____

I'm grateful for: _____

_____

Best thing today: _____

_____

Date:

Weather:

Today I'm feeling:

📍 _____

What I did today:

_____
_____
_____
_____
_____
_____
_____

I'm grateful for: _____
_____

Best thing today: _____
_____

Date: Weather:

Today I'm feeling:

📍 _____

What I did today:

_____
_____
_____
_____
_____
_____
_____

I'm grateful for: _____

_____

Best thing today: _____

_____

Date: _____ Weather:

Today I'm feeling:

📍 _____

What I did today:

_____
_____
_____
_____
_____
_____
_____

I'm grateful for: _____

_____

Best thing today: _____

_____

Date:

Weather:

Today I'm feeling:

_____

What I did today:

_____
_____
_____
_____
_____
_____
_____
_____

I'm grateful for: _____

_____

Best thing today: _____

_____

Let's Chat!

How do you describe yourself?

....

....

What is your favorite ice cream flavor?

....

Who is your best friend?

....

....

What is your favorite food?

....

What are you afraid of?

....

....

Tell me a little secret:

....

....

Date:

Weather:

Today I'm feeling:

_____

What I did today:

_____

_____

_____

_____

_____

_____

_____

_____

I'm grateful for: _____

_____

Best thing today: _____

_____

Date:

Weather:

Today I'm feeling:

What I did today:

_____

I'm grateful for: _____

_____

Best thing today: _____

_____

Date:

Weather:

Today I'm feeling:

📍 _____

What I did today:

_____

_____

_____

_____

_____

_____

_____

_____

I'm grateful for: _____

_____

Best thing today: _____

_____

Date:

Weather:

Today I'm feeling:

⊙ _____

What I did today:

_____
_____
_____
_____
_____
_____
_____
_____

I'm grateful for: _____

_____

Best thing today: _____

_____

Date:　　　　**Weather:**

Today I'm feeling:

◉ _____

What I did today:

_____

_____

_____

_____

_____

_____

_____

I'm grateful for: _____

_____

Best thing today: _____

_____

Date:

Weather:

Today I'm feeling:

_____

What I did today:

_____

_____

_____

_____

_____

_____

_____

I'm grateful for: _____

_____

Best thing today: _____

_____

Date:

Weather:

Today I'm feeling:

📍 _____

What I did today:

_____

_____

_____

_____

_____

_____

_____

_____

I'm grateful for: _____

_____

Best thing today: _____

_____

Date:

Weather:

Today I'm feeling:

📍 _____

What I did today:

_____

_____

_____

_____

_____

_____

_____

I'm grateful for: _____

_____

Best thing today: _____

_____

What is your favorite song or game? And why do you like it?

....

....

....

....

....

One thing I would like to learn this summer is:

....

....

....

....

....

Date:

Weather:

Today I'm feeling:

📍 _____

What I did today:

_____

_____

_____

_____

_____

_____

_____

I'm grateful for: _____

_____

Best thing today: _____

_____

36

Date:

Weather:

Today I'm feeling:

📍 _____

What I did today:

_____

_____

_____

_____

_____

_____

_____

_____

I'm grateful for: _____

_____

Best thing today: _____

_____

Date:

Weather:

Today I'm feeling:

📍 _____

What I did today:

_____

_____

_____

_____

_____

_____

_____

I'm grateful for: _____

_____

Best thing today: _____

_____

Date: _____ Weather:

Today I'm feeling:

📍 _____

What I did today:

_____
_____
_____
_____
_____
_____
_____
_____

I'm grateful for: _____

_____

Best thing today: _____

_____

Date: Weather:

Today I'm feeling:

_____

What I did today:

_____

_____

_____

_____

_____

_____

_____

I'm grateful for: _____

_____

Best thing today: _____

_____

Date: _____ Weather:

Today I'm feeling:

📍 _____

What I did today:

_____
_____
_____
_____
_____
_____
_____
_____

I'm grateful for: _____

_____

Best thing today: _____

_____

Date:

Weather:

Today I'm feeling:

📍 _____

What I did today:

_____
_____
_____
_____
_____
_____
_____

I'm grateful for: _____

_____

Best thing today: _____

_____

Date:

Weather:

Today I'm feeling:

◉ _____

What I did today:

_____

_____

_____

_____

_____

_____

_____

I'm grateful for: _____

_____

Best thing today: _____

_____

If I could go anywhere this summer it would be:

....
....
....
....
....
....

My Favorite thing about the beach is:

....
....
....
....

Date:

Weather:

Today I'm feeling:

○ _____

What I did today:

_____

_____

_____

_____

_____

_____

_____

I'm grateful for: _____

_____

Best thing today: _____

_____

Date:

Weather:

Today I'm feeling:

📍 _____

What I did today:

_____

_____

_____

_____

_____

_____

_____

I'm grateful for: _____

_____

Best thing today: _____

_____

Date:

Weather:

Today I'm feeling:

📍 _____

What I did today:

_____

_____

_____

_____

_____

_____

_____

_____

I'm grateful for: _____

_____

Best thing today: _____

_____

Date:

Weather:

Today I'm feeling:

_____

What I did today:

_____

_____

_____

_____

_____

_____

_____

I'm grateful for: _____

_____

Best thing today: _____

_____

Date:

Weather:

Today I'm feeling:

⊙_____

What I did today:

_____

_____

_____

_____

_____

_____

_____

I'm grateful for: _____

_____

Best thing today: _____

_____

Date:

Weather:

Today I'm feeling:

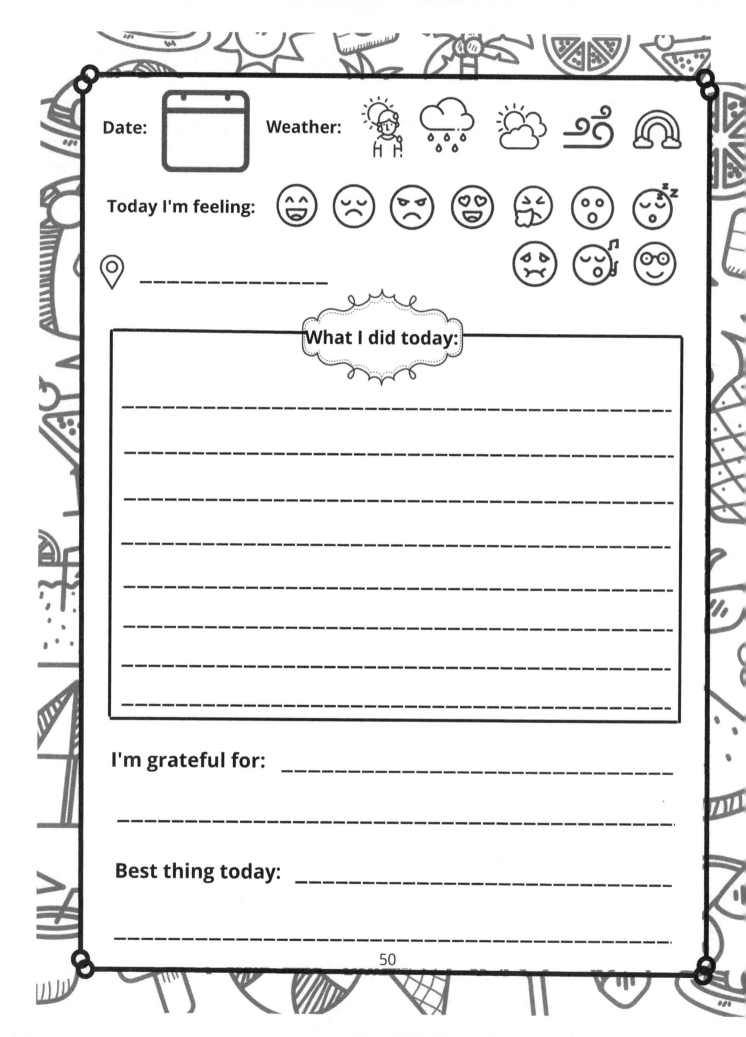

⊙ _____

What I did today:

_____

_____

_____

_____

_____

_____

_____

I'm grateful for: _____

_____

Best thing today: _____

_____

Date: **Date:** **Weather:**

Today I'm feeling:

📍 _____

What I did today:

_____

_____

_____

_____

_____

_____

_____

_____

I'm grateful for: _____

_____

Best thing today: _____

_____

Date:

Weather:

Today I'm feeling:

◎ _____

What I did today:

_____

_____

_____

_____

_____

_____

_____

I'm grateful for: _____

_____

Best thing today: _____

_____

I SPY SUMMER

3	5	1	6	2	5	4
6	9	2	1	3	1	

Date:

Weather:

Today I'm feeling:

📍 _____

What I did today:

_____

_____

_____

_____

_____

_____

_____

I'm grateful for: _____

_____

Best thing today: _____

_____

Date:　　　　　**Weather:**

Today I'm feeling:

📍 _____

What I did today:

_____

_____

_____

_____

_____

_____

_____

I'm grateful for: _____

_____

Best thing today: _____

_____

Date:

Weather:

Today I'm feeling:

What I did today:

_____

_____

_____

_____

_____

_____

_____

I'm grateful for: _____

_____

Best thing today: _____

_____

Date:

Weather:

Today I'm feeling:

📍 _ _ _ _ _ _ _ _ _ _ _ _ _

What I did today:

_ _

_ _

_ _

_ _

_ _

_ _

_ _

I'm grateful for: _

_ _

Best thing today: _

_ _

Date:

Weather:

Today I'm feeling:

What I did today:

_____

_____

_____

_____

_____

_____

_____

I'm grateful for: _____

_____

Best thing today: _____

_____

Date: Weather:

Today I'm feeling:

📍 _____

What I did today:

_____
_____
_____
_____
_____
_____
_____
_____

I'm grateful for: _____

_____

Best thing today: _____

_____

Date:

Weather:

Today I'm feeling:

_____

What I did today:

_____

_____

_____

_____

_____

_____

_____

I'm grateful for: _____

_____

Best thing today: _____

_____

Date:

Weather:

Today I'm feeling:

📍 _____

What I did today:

_____

_____

_____

_____

_____

_____

_____

I'm grateful for: _____

_____

Best thing today: _____

_____

Date: Weather:

Today I'm feeling:

📍 _____

What I did today:

_____
_____
_____
_____
_____
_____
_____

I'm grateful for: _____

_____

Best thing today: _____

_____

Draw a new place you visited this summer.

Date:

Weather:

Today I'm feeling:

📍 _____

What I did today:

_____
_____
_____
_____
_____
_____
_____

I'm grateful for: _____

_____

Best thing today: _____

_____

Date:

Weather:

Today I'm feeling:

_____

What I did today:

_____

_____

_____

_____

_____

_____

_____

_____

I'm grateful for: _____

_____

Best thing today: _____

_____

Date:

Weather:

Today I'm feeling:

📍 _____

What I did today:

_____

_____

_____

_____

_____

_____

_____

I'm grateful for: _____

_____

Best thing today: _____

_____

Date:

Weather:

Today I'm feeling:

📍 _____

What I did today:

_____
_____
_____
_____
_____
_____
_____

I'm grateful for: _____

_____

Best thing today: _____

_____

Date:

Weather:

Today I'm feeling:

📍 _____

What I did today:

_____

_____

_____

_____

_____

_____

_____

_____

I'm grateful for: _____

_____

Best thing today: _____

_____

Date: Weather:

Today I'm feeling:

What I did today:

_____

_____

_____

_____

_____

_____

_____

I'm grateful for: _____

_____

Best thing today: _____

_____

Date:

Weather: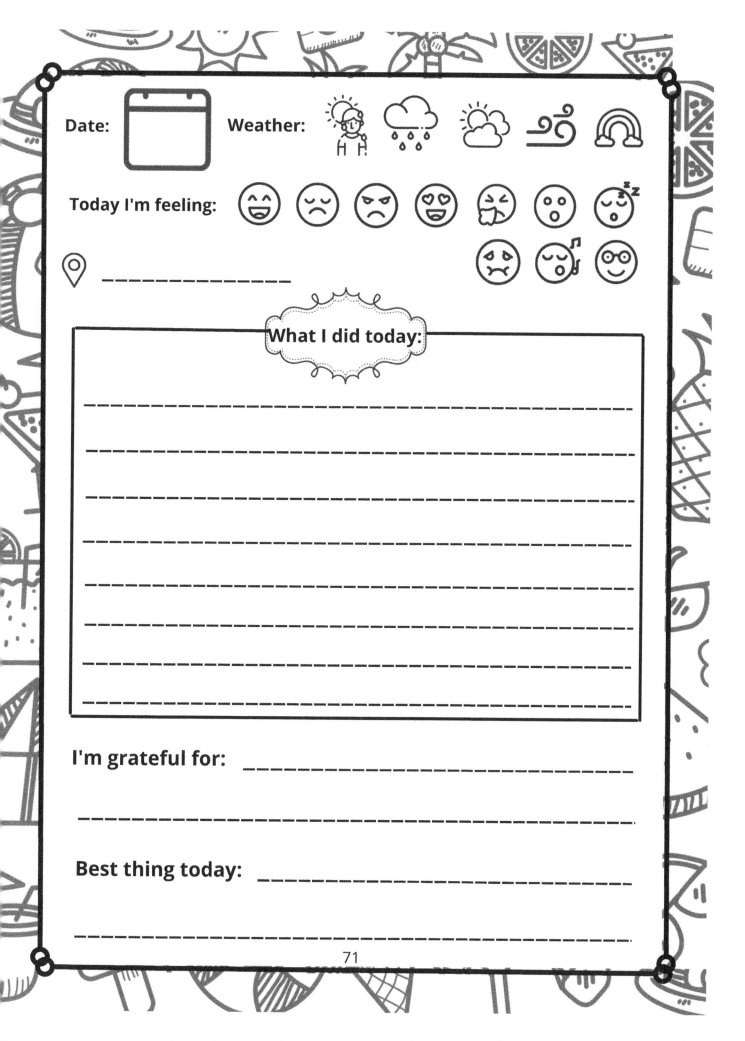

Today I'm feeling:

📍 _____

What I did today:

_____

_____

_____

_____

_____

_____

_____

I'm grateful for: _____

_____

Best thing today: _____

_____

What to pack in my suitecase:

Packing List:

_____ _____

_____ _____

_____ _____

_____ _____

_____ _____

Date:

Weather: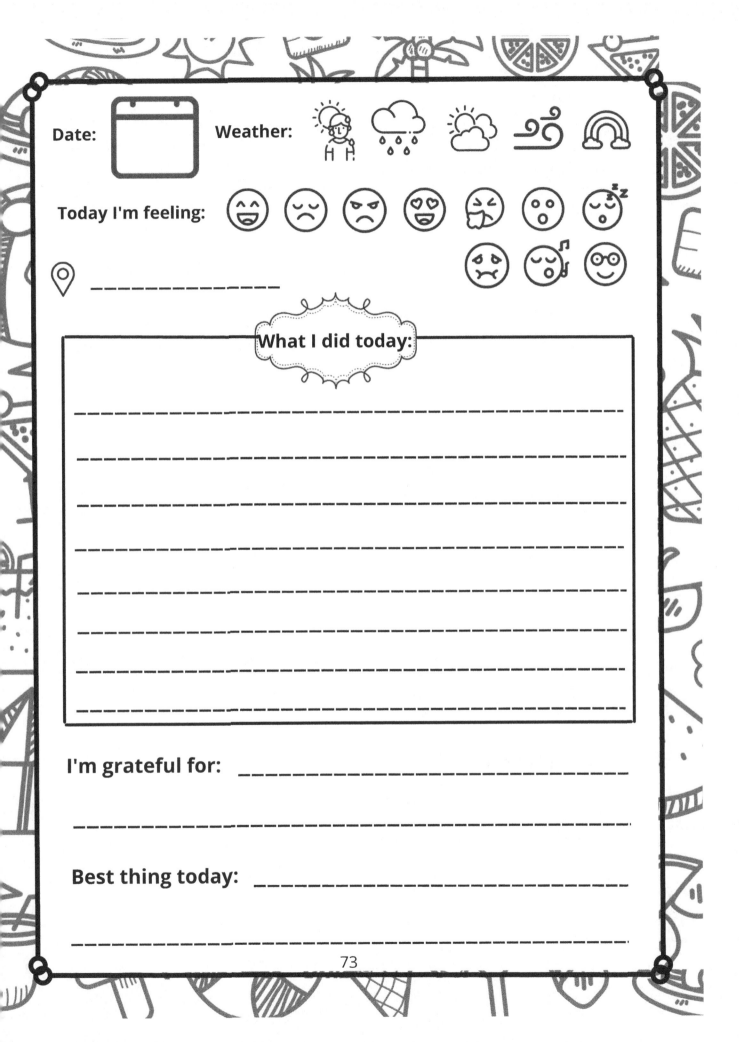

Today I'm feeling:

📍 _____

What I did today:

_____

_____

_____

_____

_____

_____

_____

I'm grateful for: _____

_____

Best thing today: _____

_____

Date:

Weather:

Today I'm feeling:

_____

What I did today:

_____
_____
_____
_____
_____
_____
_____

I'm grateful for: _____

_____

Best thing today: _____

_____

Date: Weather:

Today I'm feeling:

📍 _____

What I did today:

_____
_____
_____
_____
_____
_____
_____
_____

I'm grateful for: _____

_____

Best thing today: _____

_____

Date:

Weather:

Today I'm feeling:

_____

What I did today:

_____

_____

_____

_____

_____

_____

_____

I'm grateful for: _____

_____

Best thing today: _____

_____

Date:

Weather: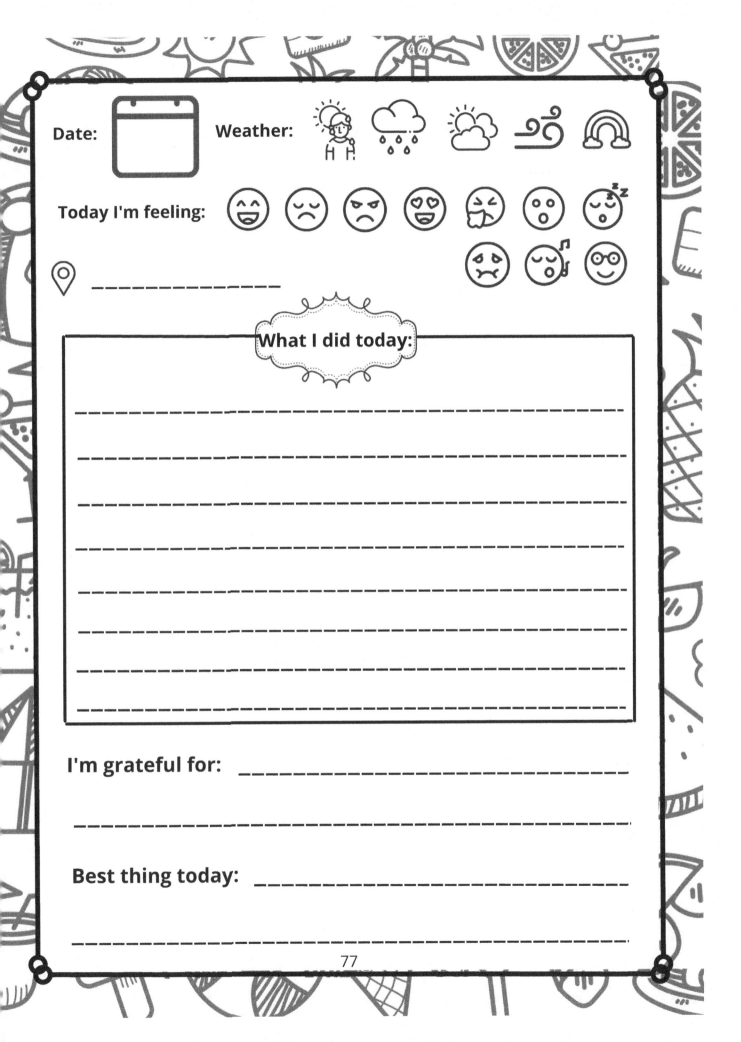

Today I'm feeling:

📍 _____

What I did today:

_____

_____

_____

_____

_____

_____

_____

I'm grateful for: _____

_____

Best thing today: _____

_____

Date: **Weather:**

Today I'm feeling:

What I did today:

_____

_____

_____

_____

_____

_____

_____

I'm grateful for: _____

_____

Best thing today: _____

_____

Date:

Weather:

Today I'm feeling:

📍 _____

What I did today:

_____
_____
_____
_____
_____
_____
_____

I'm grateful for: _____

_____

Best thing today: _____

_____

Date:

Weather:

Today I'm feeling:

○ _____

What I did today:

_____

_____

_____

_____

_____

_____

_____

I'm grateful for: _____

_____

Best thing today: _____

_____

What is your favorite book this summer? What is it about? Who are the main characters?

....

....

....

....

....

....

My favorite activity to do in the water is:

....

....

....

....

....

Date:

Weather:

Today I'm feeling:

_____

What I did today:

_____
_____
_____
_____
_____
_____
_____

I'm grateful for: _____

_____

Best thing today: _____

_____

Date:

Weather:

Today I'm feeling:

◎ _____

What I did today:

_____

_____

_____

_____

_____

_____

_____

_____

I'm grateful for: _____

_____

Best thing today: _____

_____

Date:

Weather:

Today I'm feeling:

📍 _____

What I did today:

_____
_____
_____
_____
_____
_____
_____

I'm grateful for: _____

_____

Best thing today: _____

_____

Date:

Weather:

Today I'm feeling:

📍 _____

What I did today:

_____
_____
_____
_____
_____
_____
_____

I'm grateful for: _____

_____

Best thing today: _____

_____

Date:

Weather:

Today I'm feeling:

📍 _____

What I did today:

_____
_____
_____
_____
_____
_____
_____

I'm grateful for: _____

_____

Best thing today: _____

_____

Date:

Weather:

Today I'm feeling:

📍 _____

What I did today:

_____

_____

_____

_____

_____

_____

_____

I'm grateful for: _____

_____

Best thing today: _____

_____

Date:

Weather:

Today I'm feeling:

⊙ _____

What I did today:

_____
_____
_____
_____
_____
_____
_____

I'm grateful for: _____

_____

Best thing today: _____

_____

Date:

Weather:

Today I'm feeling:

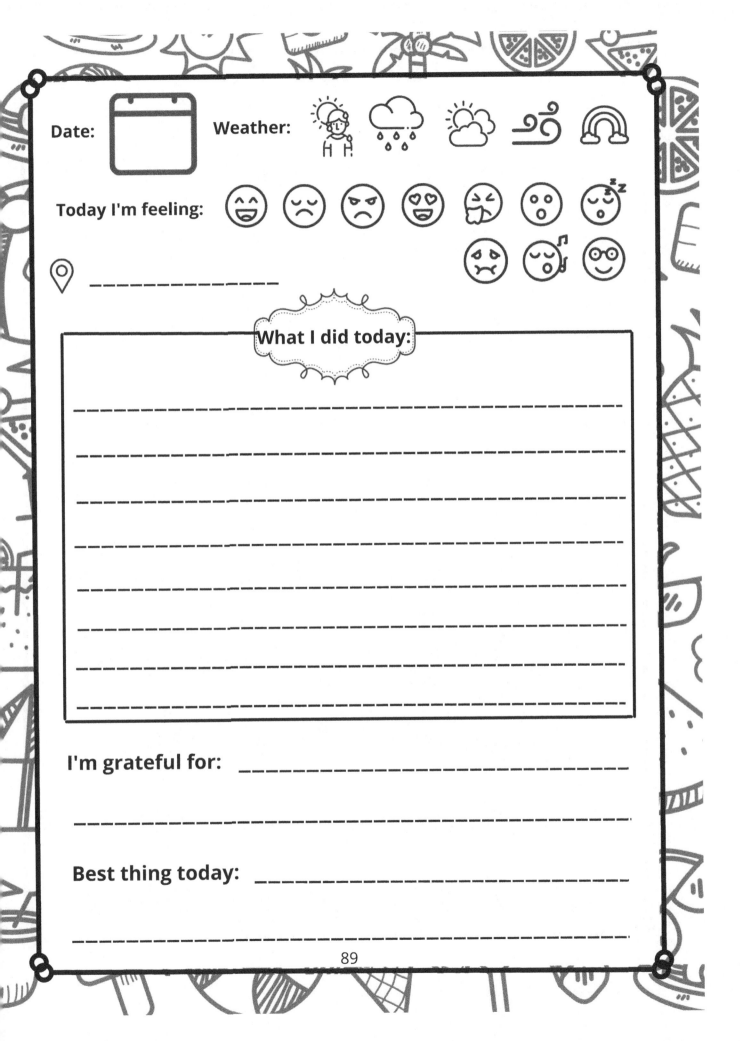

What I did today:

_____

_____

_____

_____

_____

_____

_____

I'm grateful for: _____

_____

Best thing today: _____

_____

I SPY SUMMER

Date:

Weather:

Today I'm feeling:

📍 _____

What I did today:

_____

_____

_____

_____

_____

_____

_____

I'm grateful for: _____

_____

Best thing today: _____

_____

Date:

Weather:

Today I'm feeling:

_____

What I did today:

_____

_____

_____

_____

_____

_____

_____

_____

I'm grateful for: _____

_____

Best thing today: _____

_____

Date:

Weather: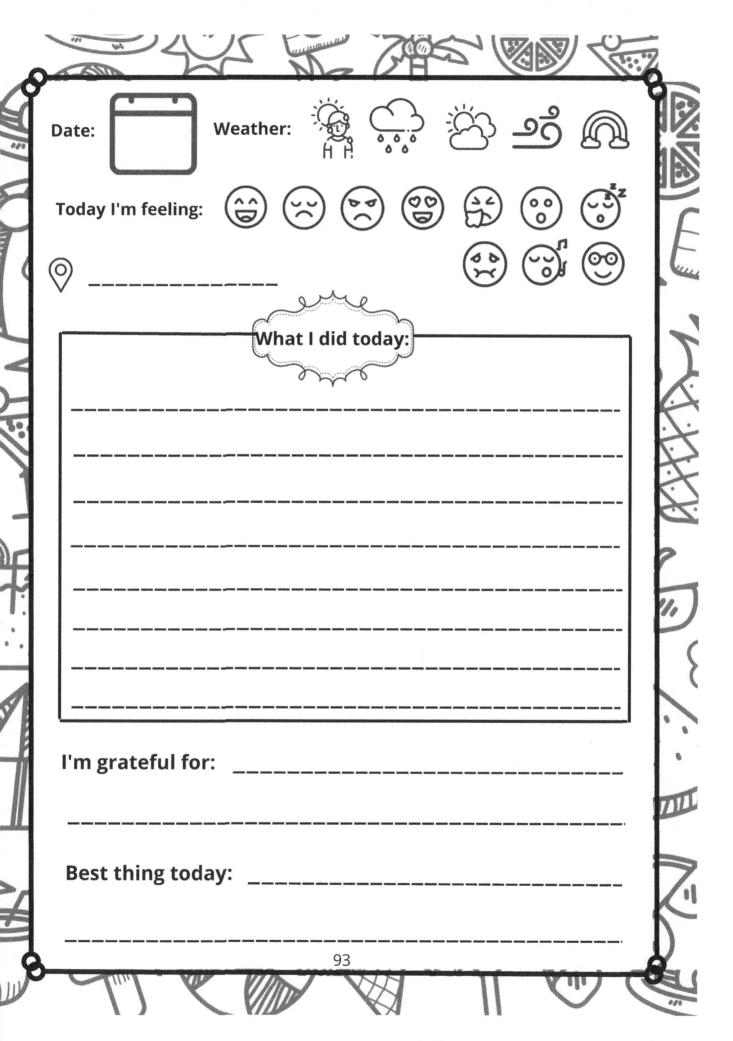

Today I'm feeling:

📍 _____

What I did today:

_____
_____
_____
_____
_____
_____
_____

I'm grateful for: _____

_____

Best thing today: _____

_____

Date:

Weather:

Today I'm feeling:

◎ _____

What I did today:

_____

_____

_____

_____

_____

_____

_____

I'm grateful for: _____

_____

Best thing today: _____

_____

Date:

Weather:

Today I'm feeling:

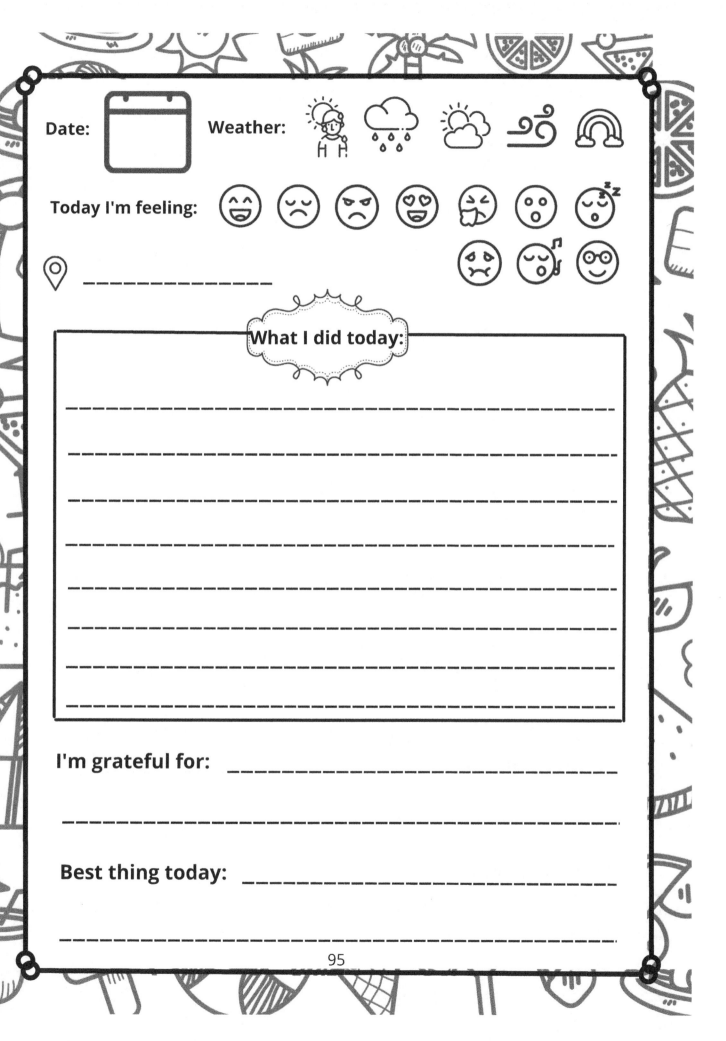

📍 _____

What I did today:

_____

_____

_____

_____

_____

_____

_____

I'm grateful for: _____

_____

Best thing today: _____

_____

Date:

Weather:

Today I'm feeling:

◎ _____

What I did today:

_____

_____

_____

_____

_____

_____

_____

I'm grateful for: _____

_____

Best thing today: _____

_____

Date:

Weather:

Today I'm feeling:

📍 _____

What I did today:

_____

_____

_____

_____

_____

_____

_____

I'm grateful for: _____

_____

Best thing today: _____

_____

 # My Summer Photos:

My Summer Photos:

# My Summer Photos:

Made in the USA
Monee, IL
17 June 2022

98180140R00057